Spotted Glass

Maya Walker

BookLeaf Publishing

India | USA | UK

Presentation by *BookLeaf Publishing*

Web: www.bookleafpub.com

E-mail: info@bookleafpub.com

ISBN: 9789360947965

First edition 2024

*This book is dedicated to my sister Melanie.
Her unwavering support gives me the
courage to write. Thanks Mel!*

My Father's Garden

When I was young,
my father had a garden.
When I was young,
my father had a garden.
My father had everyone's garden,
and they thanked him for the privilege.

My father grew tomatoes in his garden.
He grew zucchini. He grew corn.
He grew snap peas in his garden,
and pumpkins that withered on the vine

I stamped my feet
to scare away snakes.
My sister Mel tended the corn.
"Feel that cool breeze?"
He called from the shade.
And the sting of sweat blurred the sun.

When I was young,
My father had a garden
When I was young
My father had a garden
My father had everyone's garden
And they thanked him for the privilege.

A Fun Assignment

When I was in fifth grade,
a substitute teacher
gave us what she promised
would be a fun assignment.
She asked us to write
what our lives would be like
in the antebellum South.

I was the only biracial child.

When I told her my about my family,
she was stumped.
I asked her if I would have even existed.
And she just babbled and stared.
I asked if it would be easier to pretend I was
white.
She said yes.
yes
She agreed.
yes
She liked that. What a great idea!
And yes,
she told the other black kids
(the real black kids)
that they could pretend to be white like me.

Small

When I was a little girl,
the world was a scary place.
When I was with you,
I knew that I was safe.
You did not hurt or tease me.
You never called me fat.
And I can have another cookie?
I can't say no to that.

Nightmares

Dark dreams,
the beast screams,
I am locked inside my head.
I lay by the wayside.
My body left for dead.

Chimera

5

A fire breathing lioness roared.
Her very wrath scorched the earth.
Like her mother before her,
she was a devourer of men.

Her second head was a wise she-goat.
Her tail was a venomous serpent.
She was made for evil,
and so did evil deeds.

She was a fearsome monster,
but even a monster bleeds.

Inspired

Once upon a time,
I had a thirst for rhyme.
I stayed up all night,
through the dawn's harsh light,
bickering with my mind.

Bad Choices

Jack and Jill took some pills,
they should have chased with water.
Jack started a cult
and Jill a revolt.
They killed the farmer's daughter.

Off Kilter

The soapy glass of the bus stop walls
filtered the light like lace.
A rogue ladybug fluttered past.
I remember her bright carapace.
A young priest invited me to mass,
but I would have been out of place.

I ate baklava, down to the bone.
And called a friend,
from a nearby pay phone.
He wasn't happy to see me,
but he still brought me home.

rave

9

quick dance
to the base thump
bitter pill
yum

Diagonal

Smoke unfurls, twists and curls.
Fairies linger in the light.
Flesh quivers soft and bright.

See Me

I've probably walked past you,
at the gas station or on the street,
with a satin cap upon my head
and threadbare shoes on my feet.

I lost my apartment,
about seven months ago.
Now i live in a cheap motel,
with so many places i cant go.

i am Black.
i am a woman.
i am here.
i am human.

i still exist.
i take up space.
beneath these clumsy glasses,
I'm told I have a pretty face.

The Old Man and the Squirrel

a brown squirrel eats bread
tossed to him by an old man
morning motel 6

Enough

My sister Mel is sick,
and Elon wants to move to Mars.
We can't afford a ride to the clinic.
They repossessed the car.

My sister Mel is sick,
while they fight another foreign war.
Did I mention she's a diabetic?
She's not looking for a score.

My sister Mel is sick.
She gets worse every day.
while the body politic
worries that drag queens will turn them gay.

waiting

another cold night
fat snowflakes fall on my face
my bare ears are numb

Temporary

I live with my family
in a homeless hotel.
It's not that bad really,
once you get used to the smell:
cigarette smoke plus cheap weed,
and something burnt, when we run the heat.

Each week our money is spent
on Ubers to work,
cheap food, and motel rent.

We can't afford to pay
for three people, so we pay for two.
When the cleaning staff comes by,
I hide in the bathroom.

There are no hallways.
Every door opens to the courtyard,
and the constant threat
of ending up outdoors.

Fate

Hear the moans of the weary.
Hear the cries of the damned.
At night comes the query,
could this all be planned?

Lashed to a wheel,
on a blasted plain,
if there were something to feel,
it would be nothing but pain.
Amidst grim poplar trees,
the dead twitter like bats.
They lived lives like unremarkable fleas
on the tails of rats.

Most of us look towards death with dread.
Perhaps we should ask ourselves: am I already
dead?

Old Man, Old Dog

An old man pushes his charge,
in a baby carriage:
a little old dog
with gray in its muzzle.

He slowly circles
the tiny courtyard.

He smokes and he waves.
Sometimes he talks.
Give the briefest of greetings,
then returns to their walks.

Almost

We once held hands,
And we made plans.
I used to bother for you.
When you have somebody who cares,
it's easier to care too.

You said that you loved me.
I said I was on the way.

You said my ugly hair was perfect hair.
You called me adorable just to start with.
You made me feel like shy can be okay
You showed me how to lead the way.

I was a happy girl.
Happy to be.

I miss you and I miss you.
I've never even kissed you.
You said that you chickened out.
Will we never have another next time?

My lonely heart fills in the spaces
of who i wish you were.

Maybe if you dabbed a little less,
or always told me the truth like you promised.
I thought that we could save each other.
I know I won't see you again.
Wish we could have, at least, been friends.

If

My glasses fall off sometimes,
because they're too damn big.
I think my self esteem would improve,
If I could just afford a wig.

Cosmic

My body's a map of old scars.
My heart pumps not blood,
but stagnant stars.
My flesh is infused with the flood.

The stars collide inside my head,
and they ignite desire.
Someday, someway, I will be wed,
before my funeral pyre.

I reach above.
I search for sweet.
I yearn for love,
but we're all just meat.

I was a galaxy, yes a galaxy.
No, don't bother to look. Please, it's only me.

Spotted Glass

I look at myself
in the spotted glass.
And I glare at my fat flat ass.
A Dollar store weave sits
in place of my crown,
and i am grateful for it.

Where are my curves?
Where is my youth?
Where is my rude joy?

I used to dance with strangers.
Now I cower in the sun.

I am more than what you see.
The girl in the glass is not all of me.
I will brew another pot of tea.
It's time to wake up.

9 789360 947965